AF393951

BOOK ANALYSIS

By Candice Kent

Flush

BY VIRGINIA WOOLF

Bright≡Summaries.com

BOOK ANALYSIS
BOOK ANALYSIS
Bright
Summaries.com
Fifty Shades
of Grey Trilogy
BY E.L. JAMES

VIRGINIA WOOLF

- **Born in London in 1882.**
- **Died in Lewes in 1941.**
- **Notable works:**
  - *Mrs Dalloway* (1925), novel
  - *To the Lighthouse* (1927), novel
  - *The Waves* (1931), novel

Virginia Woolf was born Adeline Virginia Stephens and spent her childhood in South Kensington in London. Although she did not receive any formal schooling, she did have access to her father's substantial library and associated with a wide circle of intellectuals, in particular from the University of Cambridge, where her brothers were students. After her father's death, Virginia moved to Bloomsbury with her sister Vanessa. She married Leonard Woolf in 1917 and the couple established the Hogarth Press, which published the majority of Woolf's novels. From 1915 until her death, Woolf produced nine novels, the most critically acclaimed being *Mrs Dalloway* (1925), *To the Lighthouse* (1927), and *The Waves* (1931). These works are considered seminal texts of literary modernism, and demonstrate the experimentation with form and content characteristic of the movement. Woolf also wrote short stories and was a prolific essayist, diarist and letter writer. Throughout her life she was dogged by bouts of poor mental health and eventually committed suicide at the age of 59.

FLUSH

CANINE BIOGRAPHY

- **Genre:** novel
- **Reference edition:** Woolf, V. (1998) *Flush*. Oxford: Oxford University Press.
- **1st edition:** 1933
- **Themes:** dogs, Elizabeth Barrett Browning, Robert Browning, Victorian society, women's issues

Exhausted by the intellectual challenge of *The Waves* (1931), Woolf wrote *Flush* as light relief. Flush was a cocker spaniel owned by the celebrated Victorian poet Elizabeth Barrett Browning (1806-1861). Thus, although the novel is ostensibly the story of Flush's life, it gives an account of key periods and events in Barrett Browning's own life, through the perspective of her dog. Woolf drew on letters written between Elizabeth Barrett Browning and her husband, Robert Browning (1812-1889), who, like his wife, was a highly respected poet.

Although *Flush* was a popular success, Woolf herself did not regard the novel a serious work. This dismissal of the critical value of the work led to it being ignored by academic scholars. However, in recent years *Flush* has drawn considerable critical attention and is now considered a seminal work in the emerging field of animal studies.

SUMMARY

WIMPOLE STREET

The narrator begins with a discussion of Flush's illustrious pedigree. He begins life in the modest home of author Mary Russell Mitford (1787-1855). Although struggling for money, Miss Mitford refuses to sell the puppy, Flush, who is of the highest pedigree. Instead she decides to give Flush as a gift to her friend Elizabeth Barrett, who is confined by illness to the back room of her father's London home on Wimpole Street. Flush is at first distressed by the loss of his earlier freedom and especially of his countryside walks with Miss Mitford. However, he gradually becomes attached to Elizabeth Barrett and accepts his more circumscribed, if very spoilt, existence as her pet. Miss Barrett spends her days in writing poetry, in reading and in correspondence. She receives informal visits from her siblings and more formal social calls, when the bed is disguised as a sofa, from Miss Mitford and from a family friend, Mr Kenyon. In the evenings she is visited by her father, who the sensitive Flush perceives as at once oppressively controlling and deeply concerned for his daughter's health. Flush participates in Elizabeth's deception of her father by gobbling up the meals Mr Barrett insists on his sickly daughter eating.

MR BROWNING

The routine contentment of Flush's life is interrupted when he discerns that Miss Barrett is particularly stimulated and excited by a letter she receives. She receives further letters from this same individual and Flush marvels that her father is ignorant of their effect on his daughter. Soon enough, a new visitor arrives, and is received with much agitation by Miss Barrett. This is, of course, the poet Robert Browning. Flush realises that he is the author of the letters and is antagonised by his masculine energy. He is also intensely jealous that Miss Barrett's attention has now been diverted away from him, and that she dotes on him less and merely pats his head distractedly. That evening Miss Barrett eats her dinner herself instead of feeding it to Flush. Mr Browning visits regularly and often, and proves an invigorating influence on Miss Barrett, whose health and spirits begin to improve. The jealous Flush attacks Mr Browning on two occasions without succeeding in injuring him. On the second occasion Mr Browning had in fact brought Flush cakes; however, Flush attacks him in the hall and has to be dragged off by Wilson, Miss Barrett's maid. Miss Barrett punishes him by scolding him and by withdrawing her affection and love. Flush finally decides to repent and to love Mr Browning as well, and as a gesture of his goodwill he eats the now stale cakes. Woolf quotes from the letters between Barrett and Browning in particular to depict their respective responses to these incidents.

DOGNAPPING

A crisis occurs when Flush is dognapped on one of Miss Barrett's shopping trips. He is held in a dungeon-like abode in one of the poorer parts of London, and a ransom is demanded for his return. Woolf uses this incident to highlight the contrast between the affluent London that Miss Barrett belongs to, and the poverty and depredation of areas which lie in close proximity to the homes of the wealthy. Miss Barrett is opposed in her wish to pay the ransom by her father and by Mr Browning. She shows her determination when she goes with Wilson to find Mr Taylor, the leader of the gang. She is appalled by the insalubrious neighbourhood, for as Woolf takes care to note, the wealthy live in wilful ignorance of the nearby slums. In spite of resistance from her family, Miss Barrett does manage to pay the ransom and to get Flush back alive. The unfortunate Flush has spent several days cowering with fear among other starving thoroughbreds, and a cockatoo. He is so thirsty when he is returned to Wimpole Street that he ignores Miss Barrett until he has drunk several bowls of water.

ITALY

Flush senses that his mistress has some secretive plan afoot. She has, for one, hidden a pair of stout walking boots in her cupboard. His suspicions are confirmed when Miss Barrett marries Mr Browning without her father's knowledge. Shortly after, the pair escapes with Flush and Wilson to Italy. Barrett Browning grows stronger and happier in Pisa and later in Florence. Flush, too, exults in his greater freedom and, in a parallel to human society, in the lessening of boundaries between dogs of higher and lower breed. When he is plagued by fleas, Robert Browning shaves off his splendid coat.

Flush senses another change in the air. When Barrett Browning's first child is born, Flush is at first frightened by the strange new creature, but he quickly accepts the latest member of the family. Flush and the baby have much in common and are in sympathy in their attitudes to life, for example in their mutual disregard for scenery.

After the death of Barrett Browning's father, the family return to London, where the couple become fascinated by the spiritualism popular at the time. Woolf expounds in a lightly satirical tone the craze for crystal balls and knocking tables. She returns to her protagonist to describe his peaceful death, and to wryly observe that no sign of his departed spirit was evident in any unexplained movements of the table.

CHARACTER STUDY

The protagonist of Woolf's novel is the pet cocker spaniel of the eminent Victorian poet Elizabeth Barrett Browning. He is the subject of two of her poems and is often discussed in the letters Barrett Browning exchanged with her admirer and later husband, Robert Browning. Woolf drew on these resources in her creation of the canine biography.

Woolf's narrative of Flush's life alternates between periods of constraint and periods of freedom. As a puppy Flush "gambols" and leaps "hither and thither" on his walks with his first mistress, Miss Mitford (p. 11). Miss Barrett's home in Wimpole Street, by contrast, is described hyperbolically in terms such as "uniformity", "consistency", "regularity", and "submission", with the servants' movements impeded by their "stringent" uniform (pp. 13-14). When Miss Mitford leaves him there as a gift for Miss Barrett, Flush experiences her departure as a series of doors shutting "on freedom" (p. 17). He is leashed in Regent's Park, so that when he rushes forward "a heavy weight jerk[s] at his throat", but he soon accepts "the protection of the chain" (p. 22).

Woolf's depiction is frequently anthropomorphic, for she attributes a variety of human emotions to Flush, best exemplified when she represents his and Elizabeth Barrett's mutual surprise at recognising themselves in the other. If Flush mirrors his mistress in appearance, he is more like her in nature, in his extreme sensibility.

No wonder then that Flush marvels at the obtuseness of Elizabeth Barrett's family when they do not initially detect the effect on her of Mr Browning's visits. His emotional attunement enables him to "detect with terrible accuracy that the tone of the words" between the two "was changing" even though he "could make no sense of the little words that hurled over his head" (p. 40).

When Miss Barrett marries Robert Browning and departs for Italy, she takes Flush with her. In Italy codes are revised, and rules – found to be specific, and therefore arbitrary, rather than general – are abandoned. Social boundaries dissolve; all dogs become Flush's "brothers" (p. 77). The imperative "must" vanishes along with its physical manifestation, chains (*ibid.*). Except for the "tie which bound" him to his mistress (p. 81), Flush is again truly free in Italy.

ELIZABETH BARRETT BROWNING

Elizabeth Barrett grew up in affluent London surroundings. As a poet, Flush's mistress defied Victorian society's expectations of women. Although a successful poet, she led a life restricted by ill-health and by her controlling father. Flush is closely identified with his mistress, most notably in his great delicacy of perception. Together, Flush and Elizabeth Barrett experience the "penalties", alongside the "privileges of rank" (p. 23). Just as confinement to the invalid's bedroom makes incursions into his mistress's wellbeing (her life is "the life of 'a bird in a cage'" [p. 33]), so to do Flush's "instincts" become "thwarted and contradicted" (p. 24). Nevertheless his "bond" to Elizabeth Barrett compels him to obey her, so that he is taught "to resign, to control, to suppress the most violent instincts of his nature" (p. 25). Elizabeth, too, is constrained by those who care for her, so that when she attempts to set out to rescue the dognapped Flush "her family came running to prevent her" (p. 66). Her world expands when she resists her father by marrying Robert Browning in secret and by departing London for Italy. Thus Woolf dramatizes the inevitable tension between the safety of a circumscribed existence and the possibilities, with accompanying risks, which a more adventurous life offers.

ROBERT BROWNING

Elizabeth Barrett's admirer, himself a great poet, Robert Browning at first meets with opposition from Flush. He is perceived by the dog as a strong and masculine presence that disrupts the feminine routine of the convalescent chamber. The reader is alerted through Flush's astute perception of the effect Browning has on Miss Barrett. Flush's resentment of the attention Browning commands and his distress at his own lesser portion of notice alerts us further to Miss Barrett's feelings for her admirer. Although Browning is twice attacked by Flush, he remains uninjured and unoffended, and is eventually accepted by the spaniel, when Flush realises he risks losing Miss Barrett's love.

ANALYSIS

VICTORIAN SOCIETY

Woolf's novel probes the subjects of society, gender, freedom, and control. *Flush* makes clear that human lives are restricted by artificial, self-constructed walls. England in the period of the novel was hierarchical and was preoccupied with categorising and regulating all and everything. The claustrophobia generated by such restrictive practices is dramatized by Woolf.

In Italy, "just as Mrs Browning was exploring her new freedom and delighting in the discoveries she made, so Flush too was making his discoveries and exploring his freedom" (p. 77). The reader is even permitted to slip free of sexual inhibitions and savour, vicariously through Flush, the unfettered pleasures of promiscuity. All is literal in Italy ("everything was itself and not another thing" [p. 79]), releasing the humans from circumlocution and indirection. A visit to Wimpole Street is a return to "confinement" (p. 92); this time it is the cholera that they must close themselves in against. The closeness of their old home confirms that "nothing had been changed. Nothing had happened all these years" (p. 94), emphasising the stasis that results from a hidebound existence.

Woolf draws subtle analogies between Flush's subordinate position in a human-dominated world and Elizabeth Barrett's position in a male-dominated society. The novel is replete with direct observations about, and allusions to, the restricted lives of women. However, contrasts are as frequent as parallels. Flush "enjoy[s]" the "licences natural to his youth and sex. Miss Mitford, it is true was much confined to the cottage" (p. 10). When Flush is liberated from his fur, and his fleas, the narrator constructs an analogy with a woman liberated from her beauty and its burdens. Woolf reminds the reader that women too are evaluated by their physical appearance, and that a woman's value is so often reduced to the extent of her beauty; she finds herself shrunk to a reflection in the mirror.

Indirectly, Woolf also comments on the loss of freedom that unequal human societies lead to. The rich are sequestered and cordoned off, keeping "strictly within the respectable area"

(p. 53). The poor, in turn, are described in animal terms. Behind Westminster lay "ruined sheds in which human beings lived herded together above herds of cows"; "the cows were milked and killed and eaten under the bedroom" (p. 52). It is their proximity to animals, in terms of their living standards, their shared habitat, and their lowliness, that is emphasised. Like vermin, the poor are described as having "bred and seethed and propagated" (p. 53). In the "Rookery [...] human beings swarmed on top of each other as rooks swarm and blacken tree-tops" (*ibid.*).

ANIMAL PERSPECTIVES

As smell, Flush's primary sensory mode, goes "unrecorded" (p. 86), its "myriad sensations" are never distorted, or contained, by words (p. 87). His life is therefore not only free of human social and cultural constraints, but is more expansive in its direct apprehension of both inner and outer worlds; for him neither is channelled, and restricted, through intellect. Woolf speculates about Barrett Browning that "after all, she may have thought, do words say everything? Can words say anything? Do not words destroy the symbol that lies beyond the reach of words?" (p. 27). This freedom is, however, in tension with frustration (Flush having, through his association with humans, become too like them to be content without verbal expression) and with submission to authority, a restriction that aligns him with his mistress.

In *Flush* Woolf repeatedly calls upon her reader to summon their personal experience in order to enter into that of the dog. The canine mind and the human mind are frequently blurred. The unnamed, omniscient third-person narrator assumes, at times, a consciousness on the part of Flush. At other times the narrator shifts away from the dog's perspective and observes, comments or evaluates. The dog provides an experimental subject for probing the basic functioning of the human mind. Whilst Woolf cannot be claimed to simplistically present Flush as a more basic version of the human, she does, at times, use him to set off human-ness.

Woolf identifies little children with animals when she comes to describe the Browning baby: "There was a faint bleating [...] It was a live animal" (p. 83). The "mew[ing]" (p. 83) infant is found by Flush to "share something in common" with him. He "resemble[s] Flush in many ways [...] hold[s] the same views, the same tastes" (p. 84). Both lack an aesthetic sense, and without language neither feels the "inadequacy" of a verbal response to aesthetic "stimulus" (p. 85).

Woolf makes the point that in the arena of the aural and the emotional, the dog's awareness stretches well beyond the human's. By taking on the perspective of anthropomorphised dog, Woolf is able to throw into relief the limitations of human sentience. Upon comparison of Mrs Browning's and Flush's sensory experience, the biographer remarks on the sparse vocabulary for smell; indeed, "the human nose is practically non-existent" she admits, and even the poet's highly attuned sensitivity is limited in its detection of the olfactory extremes (p. 86).

MODERNISM

Virginia Woolf is a major figure in the modernist literary canon. Modernism is generally considered to have been a cultural movement prominent in the early part of the 20th century. In particular, the movement reflects responses to the anarchy and futility of World War I and is characterised by a sense that traditional forms were no longer adequate forms of representation. Earlier assumptions of the stability of Western society needed to be rejected in order to accurately depict the society of the time. Modernist authors therefore experimented with subject matter and with the formal properties of literature.

In the previous century the assumption of human centrality had begun to be undermined by evolutionary theory and by the findings of astronomy, and the reverberations of these discoveries continued to be felt into the early 20th century. Writers, like Woolf, may be argued to have reacted to this by giving more attention to other perspectives. The animal mind offers a new plane of experience, an alternative perspective, to be explored, mapped out, and tested by literature. In *Flush* Woolf surveys human experience from the point of view of the animal. She uses Flush to understand more about the human world, effectively throwing it into relief by reflecting on whether a relevant experience might exist which rests on assumptions, and perceptions, other than human.

Woolf's evocation of the "infinite gradations" of smell forces her human audience to acknowledge a plane of experience inaccessible to them, but not to the dog. She reinforces this by stating that Flush knows things that people can never know (p. 87). The sensory point of view of the dog enables Woolf to render society, and life in general, through senses less dominant in humans. This reduces their familiarity and pushes the reader to attend to previously ignored details. Thus, although *Flush* is not Woolf's most emphatically modernist work, it does display her modernist tendency towards experimental and innovative approaches to writing.

The novel seethes with comment, direct and implied, on the self-imposed social and cultural restrictions of human existence. Woolf circles about the topic, darting in obliquely but accurately to expose limitations: Miss Mitford's curtailed life, the seclusion of Elizabeth Barrett's sick-bed, the circumscriptions of propriety, the restrictive delineations of hierarchical society, sensations contained by words. Juxtaposed with all of this is the licence Flush enjoys as non-human animal. When, at times, his freedom is frustrated, it is inevitably by human imposition.

FURTHER REFLECTION

SOME QUESTIONS TO THINK ABOUT...

- Identify scenes in the novel that touch on the issue of gender. In what ways does Woolf tackle this issue?
- How does Woolf deal with the topic of poverty in Victorian London?
- In what ways can *Flush* be considered a modernist novel?
- How does Woolf characterise Flush?
- Describe how Flush's perceptions offer a different perspective on the human characters.
- Does this novel prompt one to think differently about animals? If so, how?
- Woolf makes clear that humans have manufactured an artificial net about them of social and cultural restrictions. How does she show this in *Flush*?
- Describe Woolf's method of narration in this novel. What effects does she achieve?

We want to hear from you!
Leave a comment on your online library
and share your favourite books on social media!

FURTHER READING

REFERENCE EDITION

- Woolf, V. (1998) *Flush*. Oxford: Oxford University Press.

REFERENCE STUDIES

- Abrams, M. H. (1999) *A Glossary of Literary Terms*. Fort Worth: Harcourt Brace.

MORE FROM BRIGHTSUMMARIES.COM

- Reading guide – *A Room of One's Own* by Virginia Woolf.
- Reading guide – *Mrs Dalloway* by Virginia Woolf.
- Reading guide – *Night and Day* by Virginia Woolf.
- Reading guide – *Orlando: A Biography* by Virginia Woolf.
- Reading guide – *The Waves* by Virginia Woolf.
- Reading guide – *To the Lighthouse* by Virginia Woolf.

www.brightsummaries.com

Ebook EAN: 9782808018388

Paperback EAN: 9782808018395

Legal Deposit: D/2019/12603/86

Cover: © Primento

Digital conception by Primento, the digital partner of publishers.